UNDERSTANDING
Prophecy Fulfillment

The Great Apostasy, Babylon, Mystery Babylon & the Reign of Christ

Frank N. Mitchell

This UNDERSTANDING booklet is part of a series
of booklets on key issues of our time on the Reign of
Christ at
www.ashiningcityonahill.org
www.reignofchrist.org
All booklets are available at amazon.com

September 2018

UNDERSTANDING
Prophecy Fulfillment
The Great Apostasy,
Babylon, Mystery Babylon &
the Reign of Christ

Bible prophecy is probably, by far, the most controversial topic one can discuss in churches today. Why? **All non-apostate Christians agree** on the Atoning work of Christ and on the bodily Resurrection of Christ, and they agree that at some point in history Christ will return in the clouds just as He left this Earth almost 2000 years ago. (Acts 1:11, 1 Thessalonians 4:17)

However, where great disagreements come in are over many of the *non-essentials* of the faith concerning prophecy and concerning the exact timing of Christ's return. On the point of the time of Christ's return, some hold it will be *before* a thousand-year Kingdom Era on Earth. They are called premillennialists (pre meaning before). Others hold it will be *after* a thousand-year Kingdom Era on Earth. They are called postmillennialists (post meaning after). Still others hold there will be *no* thousand-year worldwide Kingdom Era on Earth at all, and Christ simply returns at some point in history, and there is a Final Judgment at that time, and we then go into eternity. These people are often called amillennialists (a meaning no).

Historically, most Christians were, in fact, amillennialists, and to this day many people in the Calvinist tradition still hold to this view. However, after John Calvin, John Wesley will hold to the postmillennialist view, and to this day Methodists and many other Christians are postmillennialists, and in the last 150 to 200 years, many conservative Christians have embraced the premillennialist view based on their particular interpretations of specific prophecies concerning Christ's return, which they feel (rightly or wrongly) were not adequately or properly appreciated by earlier Christians whether they were amillennialists or postmillennialists.

It has been my experience that no matter which of the three views one holds to, it is almost impossible for a person to be talked out of their position. Why is this? The answer is there are strong prophecies concerning the timing of Christ's return that seem almost without question to assert each of the three views, especially when those prophecies are taken alone. Having said this, there are, interestingly, prophecies concerning **the End Times** that all three views **_tend to agree upon_**, and this is of huge importance because these prophecies deal with key Bible events in history.

Key Bible Prophecies in History
These important and central end-time prophecies that almost all Christians in a general (not specific) sort of way tend to agree upon are prophecies about **the Great Apostasy, the man of lawlessness, Babylon,**

Mystery Babylon, and even much about a possible Reign of Christ or, that is to say, the Kingdom of God come on Earth in its fullest manifestation.

I would like to look at each of these prophecies in turn because it is my personal view that all of these above end-time prophecies are being fulfilled, to one degree or another, at this hour in our midst, and if so, we stand at the end of the Church Age that precedes a possible thousand-year Kingdom Era regardless of when Christ will actually return physically in the clouds, as all true Christians agree that He will at some point in history.

The Great Apostasy
The first key thing to understand about Bible prophecy is **the Great Apostasy**. It is referred to in Scripture as the great Falling Away from the Christian faith, and it is talked about in 2 Thessalonians 2 as a sign of the end of the Church Age. This apostasy of the mainline churches can be associated with **another Jesus spirit and another Gospel** of 2 Corinthians 11:1-4.

In my view, *we are seeing this today without question in mainline Christian Liberalism*. Apostate Christian Liberalism is best explained by its most famous advocate from the 1920s. His name was Harry Emerson Fosdick, and in 1922 in a famous sermon called "Shall the Fundamentalists Win?" Fosdick outlined most of the points of his (*self-professed*) new "Christianity" for mankind on Earth, and in Fosdick's mind this **new "Christianity"** would "win" out in a great battle against traditional **orthodox Christianity**, and it would replace traditional Christianity of the Bible just as the New Covenant in Christ replaced and fulfilled the Old Covenant of Moses.

The key here is Fosdick *openly* claims that he is *rejecting* **orthodox Christianity** in its essentials or "fundamentals" in things like the Atoning work of Christ and the bodily Resurrection of Christ, let alone the Virgin Birth and the return of Christ. And most centrally and generally Fosdick rejects the truth of Scripture as it is plainly written, and he holds that *all* the supernatural events and virtually *all* of the morality in Scripture and generally *all* the things he does not agree with in traditional Christianity must be reinterpreted to find a new secret meaning to fit his completely naturalistic and morally lawless "Christianity" with another God, another Jesus, and another Gospel.

Further, this means for the Christian apostate Liberal no supernatural intervention of God in history is *possible* in order to do *any* of the supernatural events of the Bible. **This is basically because Fosdick's "God" is not the God of Scripture who has no problem doing the supernatural if He is so inclined.**

Without realizing it, Fosdick with his Liberal Christian apostasy and his many mainline followers is bringing back much of the ancient heresy of ancient Gnosticism (1 John 4:1-3), and this is also what is often thought to be the sin of the Nicolaitans in Revelation 2:6&15. While many today often associate the ancient heresy of Gnosticism *only* with a radical dualism of "the spirit is good" and "the body is bad" (thus Jesus could not have come in the flesh supposedly), **this was *only* one aspect of ancient Gnosticism**, which means to "know" secret meanings not known to the supposedly unenlightened.

It is also the case that Gnosticism is associated with the 2nd century teacher Marcion who held famously and incorrectly that the Creator and all-Righteous God of the Old Testament could *not* be the perfectly Loving God of the New Testament because incorrectly *for Marcion love and justice or righteousness are fundamentally incompatible and one must choose between one of two gods*, that is, a god of love *or* a creator god of justice, and this is exactly what the Liberal Fosdick says in the 20th century.

So, for Marcion and Fosdick the supposedly truly enlightened Gnostic "Christian" should choose the god (spirit) of lawless love without any Justice or Righteousness and without any Atonement and without any Final Judgment.

For Marcion and for Fosdick almost 1800 years later, we all just die and go to heaven in what is known as **universalism**, and this for Marcion is *supposedly* true "love" as it will be for Fosdick and his mainline Christian apostate followers many centuries later because Fosdick promotes a "love" of God that is **agape love as lawlessness and tolerance or license,** and Fosdick has a "God" for whom there is *no* Atoning work of Christ nor is it needed (rather obviously) since there is *no* real sin, and there is *no* bodily Resurrection.

In short, just as Marcion, Fosdick with his Liberal apostate mainline churches openly rejects the **orthodox fundamentals** or essentials of the faith in such things as the Atonement, the Resurrection and the truth of Scripture for a false "God" (and spirit) *of lawless agape love* as the point of his new Christianity that is to *replace* historical orthodox Christianity, Fosdick says himself. And it is this false Christianity in one variation or another (created by Fosdick and more generally the Higher Critic Liberals) that will take over virtually all the mainline denominations in the 20th century after Fosdick.

To sum it up, *the Liberals throw out the God and Jesus of the Bible and the sin-and-salvation Gospel of the Bible as the central point of Christianity for a non-Biblical "God" and "Jesus" based on a supposedly higher spiritual consciousness of love as lawlessness with things like total tolerance or utopian compassion or faulty inclusion*. And getting on board for all the clear nonsense of this new "Gospel" and new "Jesus" and the new false spirit of Liberal apostasy is what it means to become a true "Christian" **for the Liberal today** and for the ancient Gnostic, and as supposedly taught in the Bible of all places.

The Liberals do this by taking a handful of verses on love out of context and then twisting their meaning on unity (John 17:11), reconciliation (2 Corinthians 5:18-19), and the least of them (Matthew 25:40) in order to form a clearly faulty Christianity and Gospel message with a false "Jesus" spirit of Gnosticism and with a false "love" as lawlessness. This is huge mess and this is clearly the end-time Great Apostasy.

Fosdick and most Liberals generally claim to be having spiritual experiences of the "Jesus" spirit of absolute tolerance, but by any calculation this is a false (demonic) "Jesus" spirit as John tells us in 1 John 4, or it is what Paul tells us, namely, Satan disguised as an "angel of [false] light." (2 Corinthians 11:14). People and churches that are experiencing this false (demonic) "Jesus" spirit usually think they are *rich* and *in need of nothing* in the things of the spirit, but in reality they are *poor, blind, wretched, and naked* just as Jesus himself says of the situation in Revelation 3 in addressing the Laodicean church which is clearly the end-time church of the Great Apostasy of Fosdick and the mainline denominations.

The Spirit of the Jesus of Scripture and the Jesus of sin-and-salvation is actually ***not*** in the false church of total tolerance and lawlessness, but standing outside, knocking on the door to come in so that He may have ***true* spiritual fellowship** with them!!! The Laodicean church's lukewarmness is really more a matter of Liberal lawless tolerance and no commitment to anything than a mere lack of passion as is usually thought. The way to get the false "Jesus" spirit out of these churches is to bring in **a true and orthodox Jesus and Gospel message of sin-and-salvation** and to kick out the false "Jesus" spirit and false "Gospel" message of open-minded tolerance and agape love as lawlessness.

The Man of Lawlessness
A second major aspect of end-time prophecy in Second Thessalonians 2 is about **the man of lawlessness** who is generally seen by most Bible commentators to be a political figure who presents himself in the Temple showing himself to be God.

At first glance this sounds like the Temple in Jerusalem, and a political figure must walk in and say, "I am God," but in reality Bible commentators from the earliest days of the Church (such as Augustine) have said this is probably not the right interpretation. In Scripture, the Body of Christ or the whole of the Church is known as "the temple" of God as in 1 Peter 2 and Ephesians 2:19-22, with Christ as "the chief cornerstone."

This means, in this interpretation, the anti-Christ man of lawlessness (anti meaning here both false and against) presents himself before believers in the Body of Christ both as a political figure and as "God." But in our times what does this mean?

It would seem we have basically a political figure deceiving many (Matthew 24:24 and 2 Thessalonians 2) with a lawless humanism where **man is God**. Humanistic political theories whether atheism or Liberalism all have political theories based on *no* Higher Moral Law of the moral "Laws of Nature and of Nature's God" of Jefferson and the American founders, *and* all have, in effect, man as God, as the whole point of their humanism (says Augustine famously in his *The City of God*).

Indeed, as with Gnosticism, this *moral lawlessness is the whole point of all theories of atheistic humanism as well as all theories of faulty theism such as the lawless Liberalism and tolerance of today's Democrat Party or the lawless love "Jesus" spirit of the Laodicean church in the Great Apostasy.*

In fact, both Jesus (Matthew 24:24) and John (1 John 2:18) tell us there are *many* Antichrists! What does this mean? It means anti-Christ (in spirit) and lawless no Higher Moral Law politicians are a typology. Any politician who presents himself before Christians advocating any sort of lawless atheistic or Liberal humanism is of an "anti-Christ" spirit by type and is therefore an Antichrist, but he is probably not the last great final Antichrist figure before the Church Age comes to an end.

It is important to note in these cases that the idea of "anti-Christ" means "false-Christ" as well as "against-Christ" (both of which are the case with any false Christ spirit of moral lawlessness).

Babylon and Mystery Babylon
So, anti-Christ figures generally and the final great Antichrist in particular deceive many with unrighteousness (2 Thessalonians 2:9-12) or, that is, with a lawless-hedonism or lawless-love deception because these deceived people had "pleasure in unrighteousness" (moral lawlessness) *or* they did not love the truth of the Bible Gospel that "they might be saved," such as in the Laodicean church, which foolishly as the Church of the end-time Great Apostasy endorses **a one-world humanistic government (called Babylon in Revelation)** *because* the apostate Church is deceived into thinking this end-time, tyrannical, totalitarian one-world government (of humanistic lawlessness of the lawless one) is a great thing. At this point the end-time apostate Church becomes **the Whore of Babylon** or **Mystery Babylon** (that is, religious not political Babylon of Revelation 17:5).

In short, **the Church of the Great Apostasy (which embraces the one-world, tyrannical, totalitarian humanist political system of Babylon) is called**

Mystery Babylon or the Whore of Babylon. In fact, this is Bible Prophecy 101 that virtually all Christians (to my knowledge) have always embraced. Mystery Babylon or the Whore of Babylon is, in essence, humanistic *religious* Babylon supporting humanistic *political* Babylon, which is a one-world tyrannical government that tries to control everything we buy, sell, do, say or even think, just as is common today with humanistic, totalitarian, politically correct states generally.

Further, the apostate Church as Mystery Babylon or the Whore of Babylon embraces and advocates a one-world religion, which is, in essence, getting all religions to embrace the false Gnostic Christianity of love and tolerance as lawlessness with a universal brotherhood of man and a universal fatherhood of God in order, supposedly, to fulfill man's spiritual needs. However, **in truth man's spiritual needs are met only in the Christ of Scripture, which is the Christ of a sin-and-salvation Gospel message and not a love as lawlessness message.**

Prophecy Fulfillment

If you do not know that all of these prophecies are being fulfilled in our midst today, you probably have not had access to a newspaper or the internet for the last ten to twenty years. Why do I say this? Well, as we have seen, Fosdick's clearly apostate lawless Christian Liberalism or total tolerance and utopian compassion has been in high gear for almost a hundred years, and it has taken over almost every major Christian denomination with this new Gospel and new Jesus (of tolerance and unity and agape love as lawlessness with a universal brotherhood of all mankind, etc.).

Even Vatican II in the 1960s embraced all religions as doing essentially the same thing, with Christianity being simply the best of the lot. This is just as the Protestant World Council of Churches had previously done a decade or so earlier. I personally know of only a handful of Christian denominations that do not say all religions worship the same God but by a different name. This confusion and spiritual deception, as a fact, is absurd and nonsense, but it is the one-world religion of Mystery Babylon in substance and in all but name in our time **in the area of religion**.

In the realm of the political in the 1970s the Christian Liberal apostate President Jimmy Carter, a Democrat (in a true anti-Christ fashion), openly threw out the moral "Laws of Nature and of Nature's God" as the political basis for our republic as expressed in the Declaration of Independence and the Constitution and substituted a selfless agape love as lawlessness, tolerance, and utopian compassion!!!

And former Senator John Danforth, a Republican, does almost the exact same thing by taking a few New Testament Bible passages out of context dealing with unity, oneness, and reconciliation and twisting them to mean the supposed spiritual unity of all mankind. If these moves by these two politicians is not straight out of Second Thessalonians, it is hard to say what could be! And Carter clearly deceived many! He got elected President!

Agape love as lawlessness, tolerance, unity, and utopian compassion is the benchmark of (Gnostic) Liberalism. For example, it was widely reported in the press that the Liberal Angela Merkel wants to fight Islamic terrorism with **unity and compassion**. Try getting your mind around that! And it was widely reported that Senator Chuck Schumer by his Liberal lights judged Trump's travel ban **"mean-spirited" and "un-American"** rather than the obvious **prudent and Constitutional**, which it clearly was and which are the *normal* standards for government policy. But for the Liberal today anything that is not lawless love, tolerance, and utopian compassion is deemed "un-American" and "un-Constitutional." These are the *new* Liberal Gnostic definitions of these words, of course.

Further, **in the 1970s *the entire Democrat Party* embraced a so-called "living Constitution," which meant the Constitution "lived" to mean its morally lawless humanist opposite**!!! And they did this as supposed human and Constitutional rights, no less!!! This was total postmodern absurdity, deception and depravity, and it is talked about famously by Isaiah when we call evil good and good evil (in Isaiah 5:20-21), and it is talked about by Paul in Romans 1 & 2 and in 2 Timothy 3. With our

Liberal, activist, un-Constitutional Supreme Court, up became down, down became up, good became bad, bad became good, right became wrong, wrong became right, black became white, bitter became sweet, and so on.

This is also famously foretold in a modern-day prophecy of sorts, the novel *1984.* For the entire Democrat Party today, one is not fit to sit on the Supreme Court unless one embraces this absurd and depraved upside-down nonsense as the ***new*** politically correct human anti-rights, in effect, of abortion, homosexuality, pornography, obscenity, civil unrest, open borders, and the list goes on and on, and it generally includes freedom ***from*** virtually all religion, all moral law, all prayer, and of course God; we definitely want to get rid of Him, they say!

All of these upside-down anti-rights are now supposed goods (often even embraced officially by the Supreme Court), and all traditional human rights of the Declaration, Constitution, and Higher Moral Law are supposed evils, or so ***all*** the Liberals, Democrats, and humanists tell us.

This new political rights system of government of Babylon (that is, humanism) is to be implemented worldwide usually to do a worldwide socialist Social Justice, and it is known affectionately and infamously today as the New World Order.

In recent years it was first outlined most explicitly by G.H.W. Bush senior in his famous New World Order speech at the UN in 1990. The worldwide or globalist governmental authority is to be based (said Bush) on "humanism" (that is, atheism), and it is to have three key upside-down, anti-rights to be implemented worldwide (said Bush), namely "open borders," "open minds," and "open trade." This (as outlined by Bush) is a clear false Judeo-Christian millennialism being advocated by a truly decent man, but, nonetheless, a false Kingdom-of-God millennialism if ever there was one!!!

The End-Time Deception
The Bible says, if it were possible even the very elect would be deceived by this spirit of (anti-Christ) lawless tyrannical nonsense. This means *not to be deceived by this nonsense, one must be very grounded in Christ and the Word of God* (again, Matthew 24:24). I think it is self-evident that Bush senior as well as his son after him (both fine Christian men it seems) were not so very well-grounded in Scripture! But there is a long story to the deceptions concerning a false, humanistic Christian millennialism, that is, a *false* Kingdom of God or Reign of Christ come on Earth in all its political as well as religious fullness.

American Founders: Fifth Monarchists
The original Puritans in America sought to make America **A Shining City on a Hill**, which for them was to be the **Fifth Monarchy** on Earth in the

prophecies of Daniel or, that is to say, the *literal* and *true* **political reign of Christ on Earth** (after the kingdoms of Babylon, Persia, Greece, and Rome). Their reasoning was the Kingdom of God historically in Church teachings comes in the realm of the **spiritual reality** of it with Pentecost. However, the **political** Reign of Christ does not happen at that time of course, but the Puritans in America thought the time had come in history for them to set up a nation with Christ as King.

However, this was not to be a nominal or legal thing, but rather the nation was to be under the moral Laws of Nature and of Nature's God that were to be Wisely applied by the statesman legislator for the common good or general welfare of the commonwealth or nation as a whole. This is the condition of government when Christ is King; otherwise He isn't.

The Literal Kingdom Come on Earth
After the original Puritan founders, this is specifically laid out first in the Declaration of Independence and then in the Constitution in the "Year of our Lord" 1787. Please note: the Kingdom of God politically is not specifically based on the religious elements of the saving work of Christ but rather on God and His Higher Moral Law of Justice and Righteousness as expressed by phrase the moral "Laws of Nature and of Nature's God."

This means the literal Kingdom of God has come on Earth in all its fullness when two things occur: First, true worship of God in Spirit and Truth (in Christian salvation), and second, Just and Righteous government Wisely done by the statesman legislator (not special-interest legislator) for the common good.

Unfortunately for mankind on Earth today, we have a great spiritual Adversary, and though we do not know how it works, demonic influences can cause people to have truly nutty, irrational, immoral and un-Godly ideas that people come to think are brilliant, rational, true, good and even Godly (as with Gnostic Liberalism). These are known generally as "doctrines of devils" (1 Timothy 4:1) and in the realm of the political these "deceive the nations" (Revelation 20:3) with, in essence, false political ideologies (say, communism, fascism, liberalism, socialism, globalism, and so forth).

False Anti-Millennialism Theories
The Americans came up with a *true* political Kingdom of God (or Reign of Christ) come on Earth based on theism and on Justice and Righteousness (of the moral "Laws of Nature and of Nature's God") and on free sovereign states (with consent of the governed as in the Declaration of Independence), and no sooner had they done this than less than a hundred years later Karl Marx comes up an anti-millennialism (anti here again meaning both false and against), and it will set the pattern for

every false humanistic anti-millennialism that follows him.

Each false millennialism that follows that of Marx will all start with atheistic humanism, that is, man not God is the measure of all things, making man in essence "God," just as the man of (moral) lawlessness in the Temple. And after this humanist or atheist foundation (not theist foundation as the American founders' true millennialism), Marx creates **three counter components** for the three components of true millennialism, which are **Justice, Righteousness, and free sovereign states** with the consent of the governed.

For Justice Marx substitutes an anti-Justice of communism (with no private property, free enterprise, etc.), and for personal Righteousness and traditional family values Marx substitutes humanistic hedonism and children belong to the state, and for free sovereign states with the consent of the governed Marx substitutes a global world authority over the nations with no consent of the governed. This was to be a dehumanizing hell on Earth with no true rights and liberties for anyone, but it is the Marxist anti-millennialism dream come true in Russia in 1917.

The Cold War was an ideological war between the **true Judeo-Christian millennialism** of the American founders (most famously and forcefully advocated in our time by Ronald Reagan) against the **false humanistic anti-millennialism** of Marx.

After the Soviet Union implodes, President G.H.W. Bush in 1990 does *not* say let's now promote worldwide a true Shining City on a Hill of Judeo-Christian millennialism with Liberty and Justice for all, but rather for whatever his misguided, ill-advised reasons Bush senior says, incredibly, since the Cold War is over we need a whole new model for world order, and this becomes Bush's famous "New World Order." But **Bush's New World Order is just a re-done humanistic anti-millennialism** as a variation on that of Marx! It had been reported in the press that Bush was on prescription drugs, and if so, this may explain how influenced he was by them!

In the end, it does not matter if the President is getting high on legal or illegal drugs, the results are the same: Bush wound up with a new vision for the world, and it was a new humanistic anti-millennialism, but Marx before Bush had set the pattern for all humanistic anti-millennialisms that would follow him.

Bush, as Marx, openly bases his New World Order anti-millennialism on "humanism," and he has for its three components not Justice but the injustice of "open trade," which sounds nice but it is for Bush the injustice of crony-capitalist trade deals (as NAFTA, TPP, etc.), and for Righteousness Bush has "open minds" which is classic humanistic hedonism, and for free sovereign states with the consent of the governed Bush has "open borders," which clearly means no sovereign states, but rather all nations will inevitably be under an unelected globalist governmental authority (of an elite political class) with, obviously, no consent of the governed by anybody in any nation of the world.

G.H.W. Bush essentially asserted a particular humanistic globalist anti-millennialism of crony capitalism (sometimes associated with neo-fascism of large multinational corporations), and this is very similar to the humanistic globalist anti-millennialism of the European Union, but it is *not* the same anti-millennialism of **the Liberal left politicians** who have their own particular humanistic globalist anti-millennialism based on their Gnostic values of unity, tolerance, utopian compassion, inclusion, and agape love as lawlessness. However, Liberal apostate Christians and their false millennialism follow the same anti pattern set down by the humanist-atheist Marx, and understandably so since Christian Liberalism and its bizarre one-world religion are a form of humanism with "another Jesus" and "another Gospel" and even another "God."

Jimmy Carter actually outlines almost all of the Liberal millennialism nuttiness in his book *Our Endangered Values* where he holds that all of the upside-down rights of the Liberal based on agape love as moral lawlessness (on a whole range of issues such as immigration, etc.) are ***supposedly*** traditional American and Constitutional values (of all things), and when these upside-down, utopian, and lawless values and rights are applied worldwide we will have a Liberal millennialism come on Earth! (This stuff is so crazy, you cannot make it up.)

Carter's clearly **false humanistic anti-millennialism** is the same dang humanist song third or fourth verse. The false theism of Gnostic Liberalism is a form of humanism for its foundation, and for Justice it substitutes an unjust or false charity of the welfare state, and for Righteousness it substitutes moral tolerance, and for free sovereign states with the consent of the governed it substitutes, yet again, an unelected globalist authority (of some sort, usually the UN) to solve the world's political, economic, education, and environmental problems, etc., etc., etc.

Barack Obama's Black Liberation Theology is yet another humanistic anti-millennialism globalism, this time based on race and Neo-Marxist Social Justice. Liberation Theology generally is a non-violent Neo-Marxism to redistribute all of the world's wealth to make us all equal with the injustice of what they call Social, Economic or Distributive Justice, and they substitute that false Social Justice for classical Justice, and for Righteousness they substitute hedonism in abortion and homosexuality (and so forth) as the new morality, and in place of free sovereign states we are to have a tyrannical, all-controlling, unelected, global UN authority to implement all of this nonsense with its (false) anti-rights and (false) anti-millennialism.

All of this in Obama is virtually identical to the UN's Agenda 21 and Agenda 2030, and this is presumably why the truly confused Liberation-Theology advocates, Obama and Pope Francis, embraced the humanistic anti-millennialism of Agenda 2030 so wholeheartedly in October of 2015, quite possibly the high-water mark in all history of globalist false millennialism. (Again, this stuff is so crazy, you cannot make it up.)

The truth is we are *all* humans, and we can *all* screw up, and we can *all* be demonically deceived with total doctrinal and ideological nonsense, so I am throwing *no* stones here! Bush was on drugs apparently; the Liberals such as Carter, Danforth, Merkel, and Schumer are tolerance, unity, utopian compassion and love as lawlessness Gnostics; and Francis, Obama and Jeremiah Wright are race-based Neo-Marxist Black Liberation Theology silliness. It is all very tragic really.

But I ask you, dear reader, what is your excuse for rejecting and not embracing the true Kingdom of God come on Earth as the American founders envisioned it?

The True Kingdom Come on Earth
It is all so very simple: **The true Kingdom of God come on Earth as prophesied in the Bible**

amounts to two very straightforward things: 1.) Accepting the Atoning work of Christ for one's self by believing on Christ and receiving him into your heart and then committing to follow Him all the days of your life in personal Righteousness and Right living and working to 2.) establish the government in Justice based on the moral Laws of Nature and of Nature's God, Wisely applied by the statesman legislator for the common good or general welfare of the republic or commonwealth.

If you are good with these two things and truly committed to them, you are **a true follower of Christ** *and* **a true soldier in the Lord's army** as we battle worldwide as true Fifth Monarchists both **to evangelize** the whole world into true worship of God in Spirit and Truth and **to spread** into all nations this millennial vision of Liberty and Justice for all in good government.

===

Other booklets on the Reign of Christ in this UNDERSTANDING Series:

UNDERSTANDING Prophecy Fulfillment:
The Great Apostasy, Babylon, Mystery Babylon & the Reign of Christ

This little booklet gives an overview of the central major prophecies concerning the possible soon coming Reign of Christ. Specifically these are the prophecies of the Great Apostasy, Babylon, Mystery Babylon, and the man of lawlessness. These prophecies are seen as fulfilled in the false millennial visions of Marx and of the New World Order of UN Agenda 21 and Agenda 2030 and in the Liberal World Council of Churches.

UNDERSTANDING All Bible Prophecy:
Genesis to Revelation

This booklet holds that all prophecy should be interpreted in terms of the larger story of the Bible and the larger story of the Christian cosmology from the Creation to the Final Judgment, and this is especially the case for the book of Revelation.

UNDERSTANDING Globalism:
What is the "New World Order"?

This booklet looks at what "globalism" is generally and at the related topic of a "New World Order" that actually has *very* specific definitions and formulations that are often not well-known.

UNDERSTANDING Revelation 19:
Victory over One-World Government and One-World Religion

Revelation 19 though very controversial is actually very straightforward. The saints in a Marriage Supper of the Lamb move into a new more mature, intimate, and complete relationship with Christ, and then the saints in Christ and Christ in the saints completely and totally defeat the evils of one-world government and one-world religion. Simple enough when you get right down to it.

UNDERSTANDING Statesmanship
Classical Justice *versus* Social Justice

Probably no two notions are more misunderstood as well as more necessary to understand in our time than classical Justice and Social Justice. This booklet looks at the history of these two terms and how one stands for the Justice of statesmanship for doing the common good and the other for the injustice of special interest groups and wealth redistribution as a false human right for economic equality.

UNDERSTANDING Alternative Political Universes:
The Natural Revelation & Self-Evident Truths

For some folks as Jefferson and the American founders, the Natural Law or so-called Higher Moral Law is a self-evident truth, but for others with a reprobate mind and no common sense, this is not the case at all. These modern-day people who have lost their common sense are just as the ancient Epicureans (atheist hedonists) while modern-day Liberals are just as ancient Gnostics with their false enlightenment and false morality. Understand these things, and you will pretty well understand Alternative Political Universes.

UNDERSTANDING Illegal Immigration:
The Wall and All It Stands For

"The Wall" of Donald Trump stands for many larger issues from exposing hypocrisy among professional politicians to ending globalism, open borders, and the often total lawlessness of our time. Lawlessness of the Liberal and atheist-humanist is, in fact, the spirit of anti-Christ.

UNDERSTANDING The Whole Counsel of the Kingdom:
The Central Message of Jesus and Paul

Both Jesus and Paul preached a Whole Counsel of the Kingdom message, but this is not a generally well-known truth. This booklet looks at the concept of a Whole Counsel of the Kingdom Christianity and what it entails, namely, true worship of God in Spirit and Truth as well as Just and Righteous government.

UNDERSTANDING Spiritual Warfare:
Satan as a Roaring Lion

Scripture tells us that Satan goes about like a roaring lion seeking whom he may devour, but this is generally not a very understood warning, and tragically many people, if not devoured completely, get an arm or leg eaten (so to speak). To be forewarned is to be forearmed. This booklet deals with ways to recognize and deal with demons.

===

All of the above booklets are part of a series on key issues of our time on the Reign of Christ at
www.ashiningcityonahill.org
www.reignofchrist.org

All of the above booklets are put together is a single **Volume I** called

UNDERSTANDING
The Reign of CHRIST:
The One Big Issue of Our Time
Volume I

This Volume I of all the above booklets together as well as all of the above booklets separately are available at **amazon.com**